Ascension Island
Atlantic Outpost

Kevin Schafer

The clouds that often gather on Green Mountain provide a dramatic
backdrop for the Wideawake Fair at Mars Bay.

Ascension Island
Atlantic Outpost

Kevin Schafer

WILD
ISLES
Series

COACH HOUSE PUBLICATIONS

ISLE OF WIGHT

ENGLAND

Front Cover Photograph, Female Green Sea Turtle, Hannay Beach.

ISBN: 1-899-392-327

COACH HOUSE PUBLICATIONS LIMITED

ISLE OF WIGHT, ENGLAND

The Coach House, School Green Road, Freshwater, Isle of Wight, PO40 9BB
Tel: +44 (0) 1983 755655

Further copies of this book can be obtained from the publishers by contacting us at the address above
or via our online ordering service at www.coachhouseonline.co.uk

Printed in the UK by LPC Printing Ltd
Book Design by David Bowles

Table OF Contents

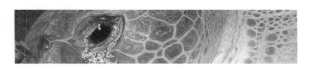
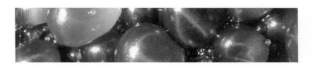

Tara George performing a seabird census on one of several small offshore stacks, which have long provided a refuge for breeding birds unable to resist the depredations of cats on the main island.

Foreword

When there is one island in the middle of the tropical South Atlantic, with the nearest island 700 miles away, and the nearest mainland 900 miles away, it is inevitable that everything about the place is unique.

On Ascension Island, the volcanic landscape, the wildlife, and the people all have amazing stories to tell. How does the Green Turtle find its way here from its foraging grounds off Brazil? How did the Shelly Beach shrimp, endemic to the island, evolve? What did the first humans to arrive on the island think when they saw its stark beauty?

Today, entrusted with the care of this remote island, the human population on Ascension has a responsibility to ensure that these jewels of nature are taken care of. This has not always been the case: 4 species of endemic plants and 2 species of endemic birds have already become extinct, and seabird nesting has been limited to a tiny offshore island, Boatswainbird, all since the arrival of man.

Now, however, there are concrete steps being taken to ensure that such tragedies will no longer occur. Under a project designed to attempt to bring seabirds back to the mainland to nest, a Conservation Centre has been established on the island. Following this, a Protected Areas Ordinance has been passed to attempt to ensure the protection of key species and their habitats.

Until recently, Ascension has long been closed to visitors. Now, however, we urge you to come and discover for yourselves our unexploited treasures. We welcome the chance to offer all who choose to visit the island, the opportunity to see for yourself the natural wildlife and landscape of Ascension that you discover in this book.

Tara George
Ascension Conservation Officer
Georgetown, 2004

Although Ascension's fires may have cooled a thousand years ago, much of the landscape looks as raw as if it had only been born yesterday. Nowhere is this more true than among the stark craters that form Sisters Peak.

Preface & Acknowledgements

I have always been mad for islands. Two decades ago, I spent a blissful year studying seabirds on a scrap of rock off the California coast. As a result, I still suffer from an addiction to wind, waves, and wildlife: happily there is no cure. Succumbing to my addiction, I have been fortunate to spend time on dozens of other remote wildlife islands all over the world.

I first heard of Ascension Island on a humid Costa Rican beach where, in my twenties, I had gone to see nesting Green Sea Turtles. I spent several nights in their company, sitting in the warm black sand, watching in wonder as these ancient reptiles hauled themselves out of the sea to perform the extraordinary egg-laying ritual that has sustained them for 200 million years.

I found the experience remarkably moving and immediately started looking for other places where turtles gathered. Naturally, I quickly heard about Ascension – a near-legend in the turtle world for its huge turtles, wild beaches and sheer stubborn remoteness.

At the time, in the late 1980s, Ascension was still an active military and communications base, off-limits to tourists and turtle-followers like myself. After confronting reams of red tape and refusals in an attempt to visit, I learned that you simply didn't GO to Ascension Island without a *very good reason*. Dissuaded, I turned my attention to other islands and other animals around the world.

Then, in early 2004, I learned that Ascension, for the first time in its history, had been opened to the public. Encouraged by my publisher, who was similarly keen to get there, I readily agreed to go. We had to move quickly: it was essential that our visit coincided with the breeding seasons of both the Green Turtle and the Wideawake, or Sooty Tern, the two most important natural events on the island.

This book, then, is the product of a single, three-week visit to Ascension in early 2004. Three weeks is, of course, far too short a time to do real justice to a place, but other commitments made extending the trip impossible. Fortunately, Ascension is small enough that we were able to cover most of it, from the boot-clinging mud of the Dew Pond to the stark, barren cliffs of the east coast. Best of all, it was three weeks spent with animals, having sand tossed in my mouth by digging turtles and squatting in fetid pools of bird guano – and generally having an extraordinarily good time.

The greatest disappointment of my stay, however, was that I was unable to get ashore on Boatswainbird Island, the large offshore stack where most of Ascension's seabirds nest. Because of its vulnerability to introduced predators, and to avoid disturbance, the island is closed to visitors. Maybe next time.

In the end, I should say that this book is not meant to serve as either field guide or scientific treatise: fine examples of both already exist. Instead, it is designed to provide a very personal glimpse of a singular island whose history, both human and natural, make it inescapably unique. I feel lucky to have been there.

Although I went to Ascension because of its wildlife, in many ways it was the people of Ascension that left the most indelible impression on me. We found nearly everyone we met to be welcoming, cheerful and supportive of our mission.

Among those who welcomed us to Ascension and did everything they could to make our brief time there a success were Raxa and Shub Sukhtanker, who, after more than twenty years on the island, are among its most longstanding residents – and passionate advocates. Both took time from their busy schedules to share their island, and their table, with us.

Tara George, Conservation Officer on Ascension, was also extremely helpful at every stage. Tara has a challenging job, yet a vital one at a crucial time in the island's history: I wish her well.

Tara's able assistant, Stedson Stroud, provided us with one of our most memorable days on the island, as we scrambled around the muddy and fogbound recesses of Green Mountain in search of endemic plants. Stedson is always fine company, but never more so than when kneeling before a tiny tuft of native grass, as enthusiastic as if he had discovered the long lost jewels of Tutankhamen.

I was fortunate, too, to spend several days with Dave Boyle, who spent two years on Ascension working on the vital cat eradication project. I hope he can come back in twenty-five years to savour the results of his important work. Thanks also go to Richard White, who served as RSPB conservation officer on the island for 18 months and provided some fine pictures of Ascension seabirds that I was unable to get. Similarly, I am grateful for the generous loan of a superb mating turtle picture by Ascension's talented underwater photographer, Jimmy Young.

Special thanks are due to turtle biologists Annette Broderick and Brendan Godley of the University of Exeter, and their FCO Environment Fund Turtle Project, for generously sharing their time - and their turtles - with us. They offered valuable suggestions and information, and corrected some of my uneducated mistakes.

I am also indebted to the volunteers of the Ascension Heritage Society, who give their time to keep the history of this unique island alive and accessible. They kindly provided the wonderful historical pictures included here, which tell such an essential part of the Ascension story. Especially helpful were the Island Administrator, Andrew Kettlewell, and his staff, who helped make our visit both possible and comfortable.

A special thanks go to David Bowles, the talented young designer who took my pictures and words and made them into something special.

I am especially grateful to my publisher, Tony Hall of Coach House Publications, for luring me to Ascension in the first place, despite my initial misgivings – all related to certain squeamishness about the heat. Tony proved himself an able field companion, cheerfully carrying tripods, catching shrimp, and even filling in for this acrophobe in the search for a far-flung nest of a Masked Booby. His fine photo, seen on page 74, is one I wish I had taken.

Finally, a humble word of thanks to my wife Marty, for all her help, as always, and for making it matter.

Layers of cinders and ash from ancient
eruptions are exposed in this boulder
on Hannay Beach.

Visiting Ascension in July of 1836, Charles Darwin was fascinated by the
striking formations of "Devil's Riding School", with its layers of colourful
volcanic sediment.

In the blue hour before dawn, the ocean surges between ragged lava boulders. Here one can almost imagine the moment of Ascension's birth, as bits of molten rock cooled above the surface of the sea for the first time.

Introduction - A Sea on Fire

It must have been a normal day. Fleecy bands of clouds drifted across the tropical sky, while long lines of seabirds passed by on their way to distant feeding grounds. Schools of baitfish leapt from the sea to avoid the jaws of hungry predators below the surface. Perhaps even a wayward sea turtle lifted its head out of the water to search for land. It was a day like any other, except that on this day, a million years ago, an island would be born.

Imagine: the sea must have boiled. Streams of molten lava from underwater vents transformed water into explosive vapour, shooting great columns of steam high into the sky. As much as a half million tons of ash and cinders may have spewed into the air every hour. Layer upon layer, rock upon rock, the debris would have piled up, from the bottom of the sea – ten thousand feet down – until one day, as the steam cleared, a few bits of steaming rock would have been visible above the waves. New land.

This is how Ascension Island began, a fiery beachhead in the middle of a lonely sea. In the centuries that followed, it continued to grow, spreading out and rising higher into the rounded conical island we see today. Yet like most volcanic islands, Ascension is only the exposed tip of a massive deep sea volcano, and accounts for only one per cent of the entire mountain's bulk.

No one who visits Ascension today can mistake its volcanic origin. Everywhere you look, the landscape is stark and raw, little altered by either time or weather. Much of the island is dotted with cinder cones and craters, fissures and flows, many of them so fresh and free of vegetation that you might expect them still to be hot to the touch.

The result is an austere terrain that, at first glance, many people find uninviting, even bleak. Indeed, Ascension's history offers no shortage of unflattering descriptions. It has been dismissed as desolate, useless and barren, even "a land that God has cursed". (No surprise, then, that there are so many features with the Devil's name in their titles: the Devil's Ashpit, the Devil's Inkpot and the Devil's Cauldron.) This was no Tahiti, after all, with food dripping off the trees and lovely native girls. Waterless and forbidding, Ascension did not naturally lure people to its shores.

And a far-flung shore it is. Roughly halfway between Africa and South America, just west of the mid-Atlantic ridge, Ascension is one of the most isolated islands on earth. Its nearest neighbour is St. Helena, another old volcano, 700 miles to the Southeast. Both were likely formed by 'hotspots' in the Earth's crust, isolated fractures that periodically release molten rock to the surface.

Just eight degrees south of the equator, Ascension is a very hot place. Temperatures change little year round, with average daytime maximums varying only from 27° to 31°C, and with precious little shade to provide relief from the fierce midday sun.

The heat is relieved only on the higher slopes of Green Mountain, named for its striking cloak of vegetation. At 2817 feet high, this is the highest point for a thousand miles in any direction, and for that reason, it tends to gather the weather around itself; while the rest of the island is sweltering, the mountain is often swaddled in cool mist. Rainfall on the peak averages 680mm a year, a perpetually moist environment that favours mosses and ferns, including several that have evolved on Ascension and are found nowhere else on earth. The result is a green island floating above a desert, for the lowlands are strikingly dry: the mean rainfall in December is only 2.5mm.

The winds on Ascension are typically strong, which can blunt the oppressive heat, but may also, on rare occasions, bring torrential storms. A single downpour in 1963 dropped the equivalent of three years' rainfall in a single day, washing away roads and causing widespread flooding.

The seas surrounding Ascension, meanwhile, are warm and inviting, but the shoreline is steep and creates a treacherous undertow. As a result, none of the beaches, although tempting, are suitable for swimming: this is generally limited to a few protected coves, and only when the sea is calm.

Typically, the surf around the island is rough, especially on the windward shore, but on occasion it can become truly mountainous. Several times a year, Ascension is pounded by "rollers," enormous waves that arrive out of the west, unaccompanied by either wind or storm. Born of distant weather systems, the rollers often appear without warning and may last for several days.

Ascension, like all islands, lives on borrowed time, prey to the destructive power of wind and waves. It may have once, in fact, been twice as high as it is today, but a million years of erosion have carved deeply into its flanks. In the end, only renewed volcanic activity will keep its head above water. It has been six hundred years or more since the last eruptions on Ascension – despite the rawness of the landscape – and there is no reason to think its fires are extinguished. There could be eruptions again next week, next year – or never again. Eventually, however, erosion will overcome the power of the island to renew itself and Ascension will slip back beneath the sea from which it was born.

These small stacks in Pillar Bay offer a refuge for breeding seabirds. Five men were lost here in 1879 when their boat hit a submerged rock.

The ridges alongside the Devil's Riding School are gardens of natural sculpture. Carved by the erosive wind, these trachyte outcrops have been fashioned into gigantic stone fungi.

CHAPTER ONE

HMS Ascension

Without Napoleon, there might never have been an Ascension Island. But in October of 1815, the deposed Emperor, humbled at Waterloo, was sent into exile on the remote island of St. Helena in the distant South Atlantic. So do the winds of history forever alter the destinies of men and islands.

This was to be Napoleon's last journey, for the British did not want a repeat of his escape from Elba. To make sure of this, Rear-Admiral Sir George Cockburn, charged with delivering the Corsican to St. Helena, also sent his sloops *Peruvian* and *Zenobia*, to plant the British flag on lonely Ascension Island, seven hundred miles to the northwest. This would, he hoped, dissuade its use by any French forces intent on their Emperor's liberation.

Remote, forbidding and largely waterless, Ascension had, for more than three hundred years, been a forgotten scrap of the Portuguese empire. Rarely visited and with little to offer passing ships, it had remained uninhabited except for wandering herds of feral goats. It was an island no one wanted.

The setting sun casts a rich light on St. Mary's Church in Georgetown, with the looming cinder cone of Cross Hill behind. The church was completed in 1847, and remains one of a number of handsome buildings in this historic settlement.

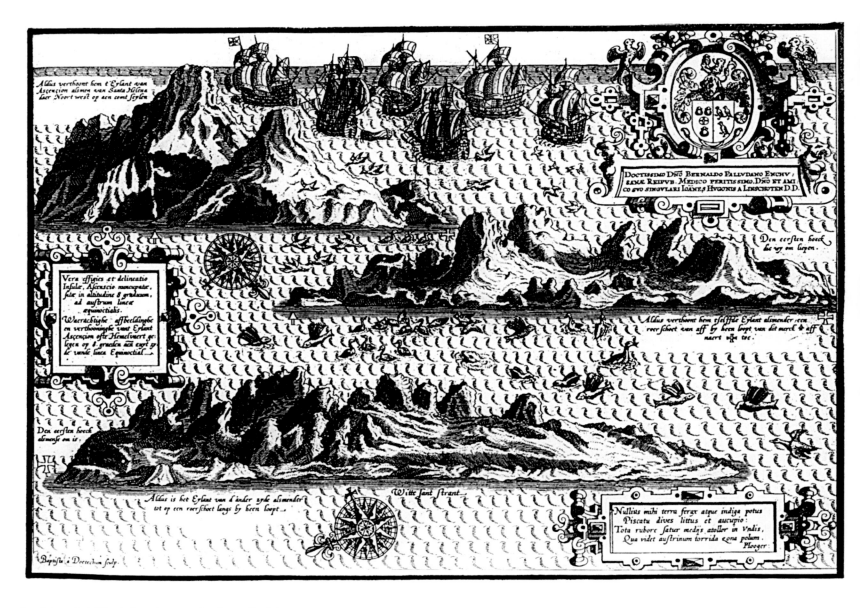

One of the earliest visitors to Ascension was mariner Jan van Linschoten, known as the "Dutch Marco Polo" for his adventures in the East. Although he did not go ashore, he did provide one of the earliest descriptions of island birdlife – and produced this, the first known map of the island.

Ascension was first discovered in March of 1501 by Portuguese Admiral Joaõ de Nova, en route to the Indies. He gave the new island the name Ilha da Concepçaõ – and promptly sailed right past. Just two years later, another Portuguese fleet, commanded by Alfonso d'Albuquerque, sighted the island again. Tradition holds that his fleet arrived on Ascension Day, May 26, 1503, inspiring the name we use today, but a journal from the voyage states that the name was already in use. In either case, sitting out a storm in the lee of the island, d'Albuquerque declared the island "of no use as far as we could tell" and he, too, continued on his way.

Obviously, a quick look at Ascension was sufficient to dissuade most mariners from even bothering to go ashore, much less establish a colony. The island promised no riches, the volcanic landscape was bleak and uninviting, and there was nearly always a fearful surge on the steep shoreline. For the next three centuries the occasional ship anchored here for repairs, or to get some protection from a storm. Some stayed long enough to hunt goats for fresh meat, and to slaughter a few sea turtles along the shore. But no one chose to stay.

Even Cockburn did not plan a permanent settlement on Ascension; this was merely a strategic move. Indeed, from that moment forward, Ascension's future would be shaped by its utility. Never a true colony, it would serve as military outpost, prison, hospital, communications centre and staging ground for war.

The first orders of business for the new British garrison in 1815 were to build defences against a possible attack from the French, and to find a sustaining source for water. Over the next few months guns were positioned to guard the new settlement and the beginnings of a fort established. However, the second goal would prove maddeningly difficult.

In fact, the challenge of collecting enough drinking water would dominate life on Ascension for decades to come. Wells dug near the settlement on Clarence Bay had brought up nothing but brackish water, and an exhaustive survey of the island had located only two modest springs.

One of these would eventually become known as Dampier's Drip, after the fabled ex-pirate, William Dampier, whose ship, *Roebuck*, had been wrecked here in 1701. Although it seems unlikely that Dampier ever used the spring named after him, and which today is nearly dry, for several years this was the closest dependable source of water on the island.

The Drip earned its name: It was never much more than a determined trickle. Still, a marine detachment was assigned to attend the spring full-time, and gather the paltry 60-70 gallons of water it produced in a day.

Just a few months after the establishment of the garrison on Ascension, Cockburn sent word that he had decided – to improve discipline, we are told – to declare the island an official "Sloop of War" – in essence, a ship. So it was that this rugged island in the South Atlantic became *HMS Ascension*.

A late nineteenth century photo of a horse driven cart returning to Two
Boats from a trip onto Green Mountain, seen behind.

The sun on Ascension can be fierce, and
shade nearly non-existent. For that reason,
beginning in 1826, boats like these were cut
in half and posted as shelters for people
making the long, hot, journey to Green
Mountain. The bus stop sign at One Boat is
a recent addition, a display of island
humour.

When Napoleon died on St. Helena in 1821, the garrison on Ascension might have expected to be sent home. But, during the intervening six years, the Admiralty had begun to see the usefulness of a base in the South Atlantic, where His Majesty's ships could stop for supplies, fresh turtle meat and recuperation – the climate on Ascension was a salutary alternative to the pestilent conditions along the African coast, where the Navy was busy trying to suppress the slave trade. So *HMS Ascension* sailed on.

Before long, however, the increasing number of ships calling in at Ascension brought disease and disaster. In April 1823, the *HMS Bann* arrived with a deadly fever on board, which quickly spread to the garrison, killing more than fifty men. From then on, ships suspected of infection were sent to little Sydney Cove, several miles east of the settlement, where anyone with symptoms would be simply put ashore to fend for himself. The garrison provided food and water, but little else.

The name of this bleak refuge was optimistically changed to Comfort Cove, but it quickly became known instead as Comfortless Cove – a place where people went to die. Today, the few bits of bare ground here remain littered with crosses and gravestones, a poignant reminder of the brief, hard lives of 19th-century sailors.

Life on Ascension was likely never one of either comfort or leisure. The island was defined by work and the unending struggle to make it habitable, a struggle made all the more challenging by the blistering heat and profound isolation. As always, strong leadership helped keep the men both busy and productive, and less focused on the hardships of life.

Just three miles from the hubbub of "downtown" Georgetown is the village of Two Boats, built in 1964 at an elevation of 600 feet at the base of Green Mountain. Even this modest altitude is enough to bless Two Boats with lovely, cool evenings and gardens filled with flowers.

In a long-standing Ascension tradition, if you throw paint on "The Lizard" before you leave the island, you will not have to return – a sign of the deep ambivalence some residents have had for their temporary home.

In the bleak and baking lava flows behind Comfortless Cove lies the Bonetta Cemetery, named for the ship which landed here in 1838, its crew ravaged by fever. More than a dozen men are buried here from this and other plagued ships – their end must have been horrific.

One of the first commandants of the island was Lt. Colonel Edward Nicolls, under whom the garrison was, in 1823, transferred from the Navy to the Royal Marines. During his five years on Ascension, Nicolls oversaw the construction of new stone buildings in the settlement, built new roads and improved the pier. He also began the practice of selling turtles to passing ships and brought in the first "Kroomen", freed slaves from West Africa, as a supplementary labour force.

Nicolls was replaced in 1828 by one of the most compelling figures in Ascension's history: William Bate. In his ten years on Ascension, during which he never left the island, Bate was responsible for a series of ambitious construction projects. Working with a talented Royal Engineer, Lt. H.R. Brandreth, Bate ordered the construction of an elaborate pipe and tunnel system to carry water from the mountain springs directly to the settlement. In addition, he ordered the building of new marine quarters, the expansion of fortifications and the construction of a much needed island hospital.

Not all of Bate's plans proved entirely successful, however. A marine barracks built high on Green Mountain proved so damp and uninviting that it was abandoned shortly after it was completed. (The building, still standing, was subsequently given over to the island cows – but proved too miserable for them as well.)

Perhaps to symbolize his substantial pride in the transformation of the island, Bate decided early in 1829 to rename what had always been simply "The Garrison" as Georgetown, in honour of the King's birthday.

Throughout the 1830s Navy ships, riddled with fever, continued to call at Ascension. Yet despite precautions, outbreaks among the marines took more lives, including in 1838, that of William Bate himself. Bate was highly respected by all who served under him, and the garrison was shocked by his sudden loss. (As it happened, his replacement also died in 1840, as did the man who took his place the year after that, only seven months after taking office.)

For the remainder of the 19th century, Ascension continued to serve as a convenient stop on the way to and from the Cape, providing turtle meat and water to passing ships. There were periodic demands from the Admiralty to reduce the size – and expense – of the Ascension garrison, but it was never ordered closed. One gets the sense that it muddled along as it had done, without any specific strategic purpose or goal, other than simply maintaining itself as an outlier of Empire.

In 1899, however, things changed dramatically. In that year, the modern world arrived in the form of the Eastern Telegraph Company, which would one day become the modern Cable & Wireless. The ETC was creating a network of submarine telegraph cables, first between Cape Town and England, and then across the Atlantic. Suddenly, Ascension was transformed from a forgotten military backwater to a key link in the rapidly growing world of international communications. It would continue in this role to the present day.

During World War One, the population was briefly enlarged by a small detachment of additional Marines, but no threat ever presented itself in this far corner of the Atlantic. This was fortunate, since most people agreed that the island was utterly incapable of defending itself from anything but the most cursory attack.

Built as a barracks for the Royal Marines on Green Mountain in 1863, the Red Lion is one of the most handsome buildings on Ascension.

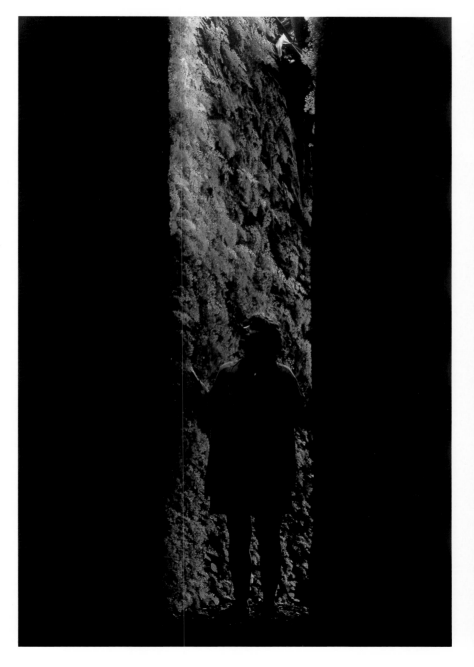

Delicate maidenhair ferns line a man-made cleft on Elliot's Path, which encircles the summit of Green Mountain at about 2400 feet. Much of this path was carved out of solid rock in 1839 to provide a 360-degree lookout for the Royal Marines.

In a continuing effort to reduce the cost of the island's maintenance, the Admiralty handed over operational control of Ascension to the ETC in 1922, and removed the remaining Marines. As part of the agreement, Ascension would become a political dependency of St. Helena, which had a sitting governor, while the day-to-day operation of the island would be the responsibility of an ETC manager. After 107 years at sea, *HMS Ascension* would sail no more.

At the advent of the Second World War, it was clear that Ascension's communications function made it a more serious target for the Germans, and efforts were again made to strengthen its defences. Larger guns were brought to the island, and a defence force established of Company employees, under the leadership of soldiers from St. Helena.

Seen from Cross Hill, Georgetown is a mixture of buildings both historic and prosaically modern. This was the site of the original military garrison from 1815.

On Ascension, you are never far from anything, and with only a handful of roads, getting lost would seem highly unlikely. Still, road signs like these help to orientate a largely temporary population.

However, the most dramatic change in Ascension's history began on Christmas Day, 1941 when several American warships arrived at Ascension, the precursors of a task force that would arrive at the end of March. Their mission: to build and operate a runway and refuelling stop for US aircraft headed for the North African campaign.

Until then, most transatlantic aircraft had required extra fuel tanks to be strapped on to make the trip: Ascension would now be their one chance for refuelling. (This was, of course, the source of the well-known pilot's ditty: "If I don't hit Ascension, my wife gets a pension".) The first plane landed just over three months after construction began, on 10 July 1942.

The presence of the American troops on the island changed life dramatically for the Company employees, who were now outnumbered by ten to one. (Among other things, they were suddenly required to drive on the right side to accommodate the many new vehicles - and new roads - that came with the Americans.)

At the end of the war, the American forces were largely withdrawn, but the runway, and the enormous station associated with it, still remains, providing a continued direct link from Ascension to the outside world. Four and a half centuries of far-flung isolation were over forever.

The 1950s and 60s were marked by the increasing use of the island for communications, with the BBC World Service setting up a relay station at English Bay, and Cable and Wireless establishing an Earth Station for the rapidly expanding satellite communications network. The Americans returned as well, building a tracking station for NASA's new Apollo space programme.

The British military, meanwhile, had little presence on the island until 1982, when war in the Falklands brought a sudden surge of personnel and material back to Ascension. Since the war, Ascension has continued to be a stopover for air traffic to and from the Falklands, and a large RAF encampment was built at Travellers Hill, which remains today. And, once again, everyone – including the Americans - drives on the left.

From the days of Napoleon, Ascension has always been an island *with a purpose*. Those who came here did so, not for its physical beauty, or the promise of riches, but simply to get a job done. I can think of few other places of such modest intrinsic value that have seen such extraordinary expense of human effort. Yet it is a testimony to that effort, in the face of tremendous hardship, deprivation and isolation that this island has persisted.

The most stunning volcanic scenery on Ascension is along the road to English Bay where, at the northern base of Sisters Peak, are vast cinder fields that look as fresh as if they had formed yesterday.

In 1941, two 5.5-inch guns from the legendary battleship HMS Hood were sent to Ascension to defend her from attack. They were used only once, firing on a German U-boat later that same year. The Hood herself was lost during the epic sea battle against the battleship Bismarck.

The first thing you notice when you arrive on Ascension is that it is bristling with electronics. Aerials and antennae, towers and dishes: such equipment adorns nearly every hill and promontory, testimony to over a century of service to communications.

A family of 19th century island residents taking tea outside
Garden Cottage on Green Mountain.

The graveyards of Ascension are awash with tragedy. Here, at the main
cemetery in Georgetown - at the aptly named Dead Mans Beach - is the
resting place of young Private Henry Webb. Although we do not know how
he died, death from fever, far from home, was an all too common
occurrence.

Chapter Two

Pests and Pioneers

When Ascension Island first rose from the sea, it was devoid of life, a biological clean slate. Indeed, from that first day, every living thing on the island has had to fly, swim, drift, get blown or be carried there.

The first arrivals were almost certainly plants, led by windborne seeds and spores that may have dropped onto the new island within its first few days. Most, of course, withered and died on the sun-baked rock, or were incinerated by subsequent eruptions. But one day, fifty years on, or perhaps a thousand, the tiny spores of a moss or fern managed to lodge themselves in a damp crevice - and thrive. In just this way, life finds its way to the farthest reaches of the globe.

Eventually, more varied forms of life would have arrived. Migrating birds stopped to rest on Ascension's shores, leaving behind insects carried in their feathers, or microbes in their faeces. Spiders may have been rafted here on bits of floating wood, while a violent storm might have left a pair of butterflies in its wake.

Stedson Stroud proudly shows off a native Pteris fern he found growing in a remote corner of Green Mountain. Only a handful of endemic plants still cling to life on Ascension, whose natural environment has been dramatically altered in the past two centuries.

The colonization of volcanic islands is an unpredictable, often pitiless, game of evolutionary chance. Each new arrival will simply either perish or persist, depending on its ability to adapt to life on this isolated patch of unfamiliar ground. Those that survived would, in time, create Ascension's biological legacy, its own array of living things, utterly unique.

Typically, the rate of colonization of an oceanic island is governed by its proximity to other landmasses, and here Ascension was at a clear disadvantage. Over 900 miles from the nearest coastline, Ascension was a distant target, and a small one at that. What's more, in the direction of the prevailing winds - the southeast - land is even farther away, making it that much harder for plants and animals to find their way here.

Ascension is also a young island, which has given life here a limited amount of time to diversify. St. Helena, in contrast, has been around for 14 million years or more, and can boast of a much more diverse ecosystem. What's more, St. Helena's volcanic activity ended 8 million years ago, giving life there much more time to flourish and evolve in relative peace.

By contrast, Ascension has been volcanically active more or less continuously since it first appeared. Who knows how many times new plants or animals arrived and took hold on Ascension, only to be wiped out by a devastating eruption, and the long process of colonization forced to begin anew?

Virtually all of the plants found on Ascension Island today are from somewhere else. Among them is this Mesquite tree, or Mexican Thorn, a native of the American desert, which is spreading rapidly across the Ascension landscape.

Given time enough, and isolation, life invariably refashions itself into new, endemic, forms, distinctly different from when they first arrived. It is a measure of Ascension's youth that there are today only two species of endemic flowering plants - although two others are likely to have become extinct in the past century. The rest of the Ascension endemics - just three of them - are ferns.

None are common: in fact, they are all barely holding on in an environment now largely dominated by exotic plants. All but one is found on the high slopes of Green Mountain, where the abundant moisture favours water-loving plants like ferns.

The striking exception is the island's showiest plant, the Ascension Spurge. With close relatives in the arid parts of Africa, the yellow-flowered spurge is confined to the dry lowlands on Ascension, inhabiting loose, cindery slopes where little else can grow. Although it may once have been widespread, it is now found in just a handful of locations. (Indeed, I find it astonishing that in this drastically modified environment the spurge has survived at all.)

Other than these few endemics, and a few plants that found their way here naturally, every plant you see on Ascension today was brought from somewhere. Some came by accident, of course, but the vast majority were introduced with the intention of adding colour or variety to an island, which was thought to have little of either.

Trees are perhaps the most conspicuous additions to the island. There are few existing descriptions of the original plant life on Ascension, but it is likely that only native ferns and mosses once covered the summit of Green Mountain: there were no native trees.

One of the most common animals on Ascension is the native land crab. Largely nocturnal, they are often visible in cool or wet weather when they emerge from their holes – and promptly get mowed down by passing cars.

This surprises many who visit Green Mountain today, passing up the Ramps through the handsome groves of towering eucalyptus. These fast-growing natives of Australia were introduced from Kew Gardens in 1847, along with dozens of other species: yew, ficus and acacia. Tree introductions like these often had more than just an aesthetic purpose; with water always the most precious commodity on Ascension, it was hoped that increased plant cover on the mountain would produce more rainfall.

Most of the other common plants on the island have a similar far-flung provenance: Norfolk Pines and *Pandanus* from the South Pacific, *Opuntia* cactus from Latin America, *Casuarina* from Southeast Asia, and gorse from Britain.

Meanwhile, anyone who makes the traditional, and muddy climb to the Dew Pond, on the summit of Green Mountain, will pass through a moss-covered bamboo forest. Enchanting, but hardly native: bamboo did not exist on the island before the late 19th century.

Some of the plant introductions on Ascension have been benign, yet others have not. One of the most recent plant arrivals on Ascension is also one of the most controversial - the mesquite tree, or Mexican Thorn. A native of New World deserts, mesquite arrived as recently as the 1970s, and has flourished in the hot, well-drained cinder fields of Ascension. So much so, in fact, that it is rapidly taking over large areas of the island.

Many island residents enjoy the touch of green in this otherwise austere landscape. Others worry that it is spreading onto once-pristine cinder cones and craters, and making things harder for native plants, particularly the spurge. There have been proposals to eradicate the tree or control it, but all the while it continues to spread.

By far, the most common fish along Ascension's shores is the Blackfish, or Black Triggerfish. With limited diversity around this remote island, this species has become the ultimate generalist, eating anything it can find.

Ironically, the dramatic speed with which the mesquite has established itself on Ascension is due, in part, to another non-native resident: the donkey. Donkeys have lived on Ascension as long as people, brought here shortly after 1815 as beasts of burden. Nearly immune to the heat, they proved their worth by hauling water and equipment up and down Green Mountain for most of the 19th century.

Donkeys have been feral on Ascension since shortly after they arrived, and although their numbers fluctuate, they continue to be a regular part of the island landscape. As such, they inspire a similar controversy as does the mesquite, whose seeds they enjoy eating – and spreading.

Biologists tend to favour ridding the island of both tree and donkey, but many residents feel a genuine affection for the animals and want them to stay. Among many of the island's St. Helenian residents, donkeys are considered sacred and deeply symbolic, linked to Jesus and the Cross. They feel strongly that they should be protected.

Donkeys were not the only mammals brought to Ascension, an island that had none at all before discovery. Goats were probably the first to arrive, deposited on the island as a source of food for passing ships as early as the 16th century. Sheep arrived some time after 1815. Both had a devastating impact on native vegetation, and may have been responsible for the eradication of endemic plants even before they were known to science. Goats are gone now, but several hundred sheep still remain, their numbers controlled by hunting.

A native of South America, this "Ascension Lily" adds a splash of colour to the gardens and roadsides on the slopes of Green Mountain.

One of the earliest pests on Ascension were those ubiquitous stowaways: rats. The date of their arrival on Ascension is not known, but it is likely that they scampered ashore after the wreck of Dampier's *Roebuck* off the island's western coast in 1701. Set loose on an island free of predators, rats proved to be a scourge of ground-nesting birds.

In fact, rats are believed directly responsible for the extinction of at least one species of bird that was unique to Ascension: a small, flightless rail that was apparently common when Peter Mundy visited the island in 1656, but was then never seen again. The only evidence we had of its existence was Mundy's written description and a crude, but distinct, sketch he drew from life. Then, in 1958, piles of bones of the little rail were discovered in a lava cave on the island, confirming Mundy's sighting, *three centuries later*.

If Ascension has an official mascot, it must be the donkey, brought here in the earliest days of the British garrison. Donkeys carried precious water to Georgetown, and made many of the ambitious engineering projects on Ascension possible.

Also found in that cave were bones of a small heron that had never been described before. Who knows how many lived here, or for how long? And how many other bird species have vanished on Ascension without ever leaving a trace?

The most catastrophic introduction to the island fauna, however, was that of the domestic cat. Brought to the island shortly after 1815, to control the rat population cats went feral immediately, and began what can only be considered a holocaust on the island seabirds. As early as 1823, it was clear that cats were out of control on Ascension and were decimating both nesting birds – whose eggs and meat were an important source of fresh protein – as well as domestic fowl.

Attempts were made, even then, to control cat numbers, and would be repeatedly over the next 200 years, but still the cats persisted. In fact, feral cats were not eradicated until a systematic programme was undertaken, with the help of experts from New Zealand, in 2002. Today it is hoped that feral cats are gone for good, and that seabird populations may quickly rebound.

Many of the introductions to Ascension's ecosystem were, like those of cats and rats, inadvertent. Among these have been insects carried in with animals or their fodder. Some proved to be crop pests that for many years were a bane to the vegetable gardens on Green Mountain. In response, several species of birds, including starlings and mynas, were imported to catch those garden pests - with little success.

To me, however, the most extraordinary immigrants on Ascension are not the introduced animals, but the ones that have somehow managed to get here on their own. To fully appreciate some of these, I suggest taking a walk to a place called Shelly Beach, not far from Mars Bay.

There, just behind the beach, are a series of rock pools that, although saline, are not directly connected to the sea. Instead they seem to be fed by salt water that has percolated through the coarse sand, loose enough to avoid filtering out the salt, but fine enough to prevent any exchange of animal life. As a result, the plants and animals that inhabit these pools have arrived some other way, and evolved in splendid isolation.

For example, there are two shrimp species that inhabit these pools and are found *nowhere else in the world*. They are small, and easily overlooked. Even the larger of the two, *Procaris ascensionis*, is less than an inch long, spotted red and yellow, and is somewhat uncommon. The smaller is *Typhlatya rogersi*, pale white and much more abundant. You might not guess it, but these two insignificant crustaceans play out a mini-Serengeti: *Procaris*, fast moving and powerful, is a predator, and *Typhlatya* its prey.

Although endemic to Ascension, both of these crustacians are related to similar species elsewhere. (*Procaris*, for example, has close relatives in Bermuda and Hawaii.) This begs the question: how did such odd creatures, with such specific habitat requirements, get to Ascension in the first place? How did they travel across thousands of miles of ocean to this anomalous cluster of isolated pools? Were they carried alive in the gut of a fish? Dropped out of the sky by a passing bird? Or perhaps their larvae are scattered all across

This tiny shrimp is found only in the saline pools on Shelly Beach – *and nowhere else on Earth*. Its closest relatives, however, are found in Bermuda and Hawaii – how does a tiny invertebrate like this travel halfway around the world?

the oceans of the world, perennially wandering, hoping one day to find just such a place. We can only imagine.

Ascension has other oddities as well, from a giant pseudoscorpion - found only among the nests of birds on Boatswainbird Island - to a blind springtail, a tiny flightless insect restricted to the dark, humid interior of some lava caves. Both are examples of the endless creativity and adaptability of life, and charter members of this island Ark. In the end, islands like Ascension are invaluable laboratories for understanding the power of evolution, the effects of both pests and pioneers, and the mysteries of life itself.

Translucent globes of green algae line the edges of the saline pools at Shelly Beach. These easily overlooked pools are gardens of evolution, with several species found nowhere else on Earth.

Legend has it that the Sally Lightfoot Crab is named after a dancer who was remarkably quick on her feet. Whatever the truth, these small shore crabs are almost impossible to catch.

Ascension has a sampling of plants from all over the globe. Introduced in the mid-nineteenth century, the Pandanus, or Screw Pine, is native to the South Pacific.

This tiny endemic fern has probably survived on Ascension through its adaptability.
It grows today inside abandoned buildings, man-made tunnels, and even among the non-native bamboo.
(Xiphopteris ascensionense)

Found only on the highest reaches of the island, this endemic fern's tough fronds help it resist the near-constant wind.
(Marattia purpurascens)

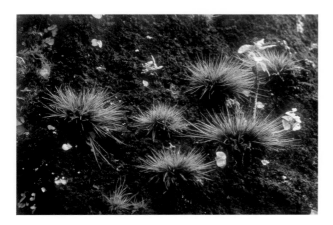

Hardly a botanical showstopper, this modest grass is actually one of
Ascension's greatest treasures. The last few tufts cling to life along the
sheer eastern face of Green Mountain.
(Sporobolus caespitosus)

The only endemic flowering plant on the island is the Ascension
Spurge, one of the few plants adapted to the lowland cinder fields.
Habitat alteration and invasive plants threaten it, however.
(Euphorbia origanoides)

CHAPTER THREE

The Admiral's Turtles

If you want a glimpse of life on Earth during the Jurassic, you don't have to go to a museum - or to the cinema. Step onto an Ascension Island beach on any night between December and May and you can witness a drama that has remained essentially unchanged since the Age of Dinosaurs - the return of the sea turtles.

It begins slowly, long after sunset, as the fierce equatorial air has begun to cool, and a feast of stars shimmers in the pitch-black sky. Suddenly, without warning, dark shapes begin to emerge from the surf, and to move slowly up the beach.

Perfectly designed for life at sea and weighing 400 pounds or more, these giant reptiles seem oddly ill-equipped for travel on land. Their weight alone is nearly enough to suffocate them, and so they stop often to rest, breathing deeply. Yet despite this enormous effort, they have hauled themselves onto this beach for one aching purpose: to lay their eggs in the warm sand where they themselves were born.

Roughly three thousand female Green Sea Turtles lay their eggs on Ascension each year, making this one of the largest breeding aggregations in the Atlantic Ocean. During the height of the season nearly every inch of available sand on the island is used by

As the sun rises, a handful of female turtles may still be found covering up their nests. With their powerful front flippers, they toss sand over a large area to disguise the location of the nest chamber.

A hoist is used to lift a 400 pound turtle from the holding ponds in Georgetown - destined for someone's table.

The power of instinct. Like a wind-up toy, a baby turtle begins swimming frantically as soon as it enters the sea – despite the fact that it has entered an entirely unfamiliar world.

nesting turtles, a frenzy of activity that leaves the beaches themselves pocked with characteristic nesting pits, each three feet deep and as much as twelve feet across. (Add to this their criss-crossing tracks, not unlike the treads of tanks, and the scene resembles Normandy on D-Day.)

Having mated with one of the males that lurk just offshore, or even several of them, a female sea turtle may come to land three or more times a season to nest. It is hard work: during each trip ashore, she must search for a proper site, assess the characteristics of the sand, dig a complex hole and nest chamber, and lay her eggs - usually more than 100 at a time. This done, she must then cover and disguise the nest before returning to the sea.

The entire process, which may take several hours, does not always go according to plan. As many as a third of all the females that come ashore on a given night will simply, inexplicably, turn around and return to the sea without ever nesting. Other females may begin as many as ten separate nests on a single night, abandoning each one before finally settling down to the business of laying.

Some turtles seem particularly fussy. One morning on Ascension I followed the tracks of a female at Clarence Bay that had crawled over the entire beach, crossed a road, wandered through a sports field, and appeared to make a serious attempt to climb a rocky hillside beyond. Confused? Picky? Impossible to tell.

Roughly two months after the eggs are laid, they begin to hatch deep in the sand. From this point, instinct guides the baby turtles' first hours - and is the key to their survival. First, they must judge the temperature of the sand above them, and try to time their emergence under the protective cover of darkness. Then, when the time is right, they must begin digging towards the surface, their joint efforts gradually lifting them upward through the sand. Eventually, the clutch of baby turtles will reach the surface, only to encounter a world they have never seen. It is a dangerous world, indeed.

With any luck at all, it will still be dark, and they will scramble unhesitatingly toward the sea, following the pale glow of the surf. But if they are late, and the sun has risen, they can be roasted alive in the searing heat, or fall prey to the squadrons of frigatebirds that arrive on the nesting beaches every morning in search of an easy meal.

Even hatchlings that reach the sea are not safe, for the frigates often follow them offshore and, with ruthless efficiency, snap them up as they rise to breathe. They must also find a way past the schools of hungry blackfish and groupers that wait just beyond the breakers. The lives of the baby turtles are often brief – as few as one in a thousand will survive to ever see Ascension again.

No one knows precisely where baby Ascension turtles go when they leave the island. For a decade or more, they will largely vanish from our view (where, and how, young turtles live remains one of the most persistent puzzles in turtle biology) but it is likely that they spend their first years of life simply carried by the ocean currents, lingering at drift lines where food tends to gather.

In this historic photograph, sea turtles are loaded into a tender for delivery to one of the ships that have called at Ascension, perhaps on its way back to England.

A baby turtle breaks out of its shell to begin its challenging – and likely brief – life. Normally, turtles hatch deep in the sand, but on this occasion a digging turtle had inadvertently uncovered an earlier nest, tossing eggs and hatchlings across the beach.

A baby Green Sea Turtle races for the sea, leaving its telltale tracks in the sand. On a typical morning in April or May, you may see thousands of these tracks heading towards the surf from the previous night's hatch.

Inviting, but deadly. The steep shorelines and powerful undertow of Ascension's beaches make swimming a dangerous proposition – unless, of course, you're a sea turtle. *Long Beach.*

Eventually, however, any surviving turtles will re-appear, having somehow found their way to the northeastern coast of Brazil, where vast beds of marine grass and algae provide their adult food. For the next few decades, they will live easily and well, having grown large enough to avoid the attentions of most predators.

Yet one day all this will change. At age thirty or forty, a new suite of hormones will suddenly urge them to abandon this easy life, and to begin an arduous journey back to the distant beaches of Ascension, more than 1250 miles to the east.

It is, by any measure, an extraordinary journey. It may take six weeks for a turtle to find its way to Ascension, following invisible pathways on an empty sea. For the next six months, breeding females will have nothing to eat, living on fat reserves as they make their way there, undergo the stress of laying up to five nests at two-week intervals, before setting off again for the coast of Brazil. No wonder that most females breed only every three or four years.

This extravagant ordeal is made all the more miraculous by the fact that we have almost no idea about how they find their way. Perhaps they are able to detect, and follow, subtle traces of the island's scent in the ocean currents, or in the persistent trade winds. Maybe they can home in on Ascension's unique magnetic signature. Then again, maybe they do a combination of both.

However it is done, turtle navigation is not an exact science. When a group of captured Ascension turtles were released at sea with transmitters fixed, they generally found their way back to the island, yet rarely by a direct route. Most seemed to circle around, searching for clues, before making a direct line to the island from a downwind direction - a result that seems to suggest an ability to read airborne clues. Others, however, never made it back at all.

The fact is that while we are often amazed by the ability of turtles to navigate – and correctly so – some simply get lost. Ascension turtles show up every year in St. Helena, for example, 700 miles to the south. Yet the occasional lost turtle could actually help establish new populations in new locations, sometimes a key to long-term success. It is likely, in fact, that the very existence of the Ascension colony may be nothing more than the result of sloppy navigation.

DNA evidence suggests that the island population was established as recently as 10,000 years ago, long after Ascension rose from the sea. For that reason, it is likely that this entire population could have been founded by a single pregnant female, lost at sea, who fetched up on the Ascension sands. From that single pioneer, a dynasty was born.

No animal, meanwhile, is more intimately linked with Ascension's human history than the Green Sea Turtle. With its lack of easy water, Ascension would have been roundly ignored by early mariners, had it not been for the seasonal abundance of turtles along its shores. Good to eat, and easy to catch, turtles became a regular source of fresh food for ships returning to Europe, from the 17th century on.

Scientists have essentially no idea where baby turtles go for their first few years of life. With luck, this hatchling will survive, and eventually find its way to the adult feeding grounds off the coast of Northeastern Brazil.

According to Peter Osbeck, a Swedish ship's chaplain who landed on the island in 1752, one turtle could provide a fine meal for 130 hungry sailors. No surprise, then, that when the British garrison was established on Ascension, turtle meat became a regular addition to the marines' diet.

What's more, within a few years, turtling had grown into something of an industry on Ascension, one that would continue for the next two centuries. Whatever turtles were not consumed by the garrison could be sold to passing ships, or bartered for hard-to-come-by essentials such as coal and nails, flour and wine. Marines were paid half a crown for each 'turned' turtle. Tossed onto their back, an adult turtle cannot right itself, and can only wait to be hauled off to the butcher. More than 1500 turtles were taken in 1845, the highest number of any year on record.

Turtles were also regularly shipped back to England as a sort of culinary tithe to everyone from the Lords of the Admiralty to the Royal Family. Not all survived the journey, but many Ascension turtles clearly found their way into the soup tureens of Whitehall.

The turtle trade continued even after the Navy withdrew from Ascension in 1922: two years later, the government offered a turtle concession to the Eastern Telegraph Company for £100 a year and a share of the profits. There weren't many of those. By 1935, after losing money for years to increased shipping costs and reduced demand, the Company finally abandoned the trade.

A smaller male mates with a female in the water off Ascension. Male turtles have no reason to go ashore, and simply linger along the coast waiting for receptive females. (Photo by Jimmy Young)

Today, the Ascension turtle population is one of the best protected, and least disturbed in the world. Not that they are entirely safe: all of the world's sea turtle species remain under threat, largely because of the array of deadly things we throw in their way, including fishing nets, pollution and discarded plastic. What's more, although a commercial harvest no longer takes place on Ascension, some turtles are still lost every year to hunting and accidental capture in Brazil.

In the meantime, global climate change may prove to be having an even more profound impact on Ascension's turtles. Specifically, a gradual increase in temperatures on the island could be driving the turtles toward extinction.

How this can be so is related to a single compelling fact of turtle biology: the temperature in its nest chamber determines the sex of a sea turtle hatchling. At what is known as the "pivotal" temperature, 29°C, equal numbers of males and females are produced: if nest temperatures are higher, more female turtles are born. Less than 29°, on the other hand, and the ratio tips back toward more males.

A recent study has suggested that sand temperatures on Ascension may have been gradually increasing for the past 100 years. Already, two-thirds of the turtles born on Ascension today are females and *this percentage is rising*. If global temperatures continue to rise, as is increasingly the prediction, the Ascension turtles could produce almost entirely females, and the population could wither and vanish.

Once turned on their backs, nesting turtles are unable to right themselves. In this historic photograph, three men pose with their 'catch', before transporting them to the Georgetown turtle ponds.

Yet, during the more than 150 million years that sea turtles have roamed the earth, their world has changed dramatically many times. Ice ages have come and gone, islands risen and disappeared, beaches created and destroyed. In fact, it is a testimony to the extraordinary adaptability of sea turtles that they have survived at all; when conditions have changed, they have simply moved on – and survived.

However, this is no cause for complacency. Although in the past there have always been new islands or new beaches, better suited to their needs, this may no longer be the case. The danger now is that as human populations grow, and pressures on the environment increase, there may be no place for the Ascension turtles to go.

For now, however, the turtles of Ascension are holding their own, their numbers appear to be increasing. Long may it be so.

With her fellow "Rainbow Girls" young Shannon Yon helps biologists release turtle hatchlings after sunset. Surrounded by nature, many Ascension children learn early about the animals that share their island.

A clutch of baby turtles emerges from the sand, ready to begin their mad dash for the sea. If they make it, their troubles are far from over, for as few as one in a thousand will survive to return to Ascension.

Virtually every inch of sand on Ascension is used by nesting turtles; here, the beach at Hannay is riddled with tracks and nesting pits from the previous night's activity.

Imagine the sensation of a baby turtle entering the sea for the very first time – does it feel joy? confusion? relief? If it survives, this baby turtle will swim tens of thousands of miles in its lifetime.

One that didn't make it. At Northeast Bay, Ascension Frigatebirds gather every morning to pick off late hatchlings. It is a shooting gallery in which the turtles invariably lose.

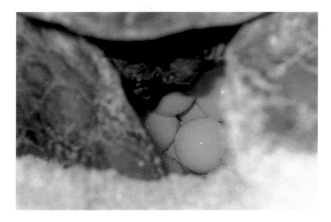

With her flexible hind flippers, a female turtle begins to cover over the bottle-shaped cavity she has deftly excavated for her eggs.

Having finished nesting at first light, this female turtle begins ploughing through the still cool sand back to the sea. She may lay three or more nests before beginning her long migration back to Brazil.
Long Beach.

CHAPTER FOUR

Wideawake Fair

Along the northern shore of Ascension Island is some of the most broken, inhospitable ground I have ever seen. A vast lava plain, its surface is a horror of ragged spikes, rolling clinker and ankle-breaking holes; in short, a rough place for a walk.

But there is something curious about these endless expanses of black slag. Nearly every piece of jutting rock is tipped with an odd white crust - a strange mineral deposit, perhaps, or lingering bits of volcanic ash from an ancient eruption?

Neither one: these splashes of white are the fossilized droppings of tens of thousands of birds, all that remains of vast colonies of seabirds that once gathered on these lava plains. They are the traces of ghosts.

From the earliest descriptions of Ascension Island, we know that the number of seabirds that once lived here was staggering. Dutch mariner Jan van Linschoten wrote in 1589 that birds came to their anchorage, "by thousands, flying about our ships." Similarly, Cornishman Peter Mundy, visiting Ascension in 1656 on his return home from India, wrote that the "sea fowle... are a numberlesse number."

At any moment of the day, the air above a Wideawake Fair is filled with birds, including one that has come to ward off an unwelcome intruder.

A pair of Masked Boobies begins the elaborate ritual that is a precursor to mating. This is one of the first nesting pairs to select a site on the main island after the eradication of cats.
(Photograph by Tony Hall)

No one knows precisely how many there were, but even conservative estimates put the number in the millions. This should come as no surprise; Ascension is the only island in the middle of thousands of kilometres of open sea and would have been an irresistible magnet for nesting birds.

Yet by the time Charles Darwin visited Ascension in 1836, these great cities of birds were already a memory, their passing marked only by these wistful traces of guano. How could they have disappeared so quickly?

Rats certainly would have taken their toll, having been present on the island for over a century. Indeed, rats were almost certainly responsible for the disappearance of Madeiran Storm Petrels from the island. But for many of Ascension's seabirds, the true catastrophe was the introduction of domestic cats.

Almost as soon as they appeared on the island, cats went feral, and began a slaughter among the seabird colonies that would continue unabated for nearly two hundred years. In the absence of trees or extensive cliffs, nearly all of Ascension's native birds nested on the ground - and the cats made short work of them.

Faced with annihilation, the majority of Ascension's seabirds were forced to abandon the island altogether. Fortunately there was a sanctuary nearby in the form of Boatswainbird Island, a sheer-sided stack off Ascension's eastern tip. Only five hectares in size, Boatswainbird is separated from the mainland by a channel of deep water and proved inaccessible to both cats and rats.

It is no exaggeration to say that without this rocky lifeboat several seabird species might have vanished forever. Chief among them would have been the Ascension Frigatebird, the only seabird endemic to the island. Although common on the mainland before 1815, today the entire world's population - fewer than 5000 birds - breeds only on the flat summit of Boatswainbird Island.

The frigate is one of the most striking of birds, with its sharply angular six-foot wingspan and - among males - its brilliant crimson pouch. When inflated, this pouch is meant to be waved enticingly at females who, we are led to believe, find it irresistible.

With a lack of oil in their feathers, which makes them prone to water logging, and with their tiny unwebbed feet, frigates seem an odd sort of seabird. They cannot land safely on the water, for fear of drowning. Yet whatever they may lack in aquatic talent, they more than make up in

A male Ascension Frigatebird on Boatswainbird Island displays its stunning red pouch to attract a passing female.
(Photograph by Richard White)

Hovering overhead at dusk, a Fairy Tern seems more curious than aggressive. These delicate seabirds are easy to see among the eucalyptus groves on the road to Green Mountain.

their consummate aerial skills. Frigates have the lightest body weight to wing size ratio of any bird, a statistic that simply means they can manoeuvre like a jet fighter - an avian top gun.

Sometimes referred to as a man-o'-war bird, the frigatebird is aptly named: he is a pirate, and the ultimate master of opportunity, able to snatch fish out of the water without getting wet, or pick baby turtles off the beach in mid-flight. And, most famously, frigates are *kleptoparasites*, experts at harassing other birds until they relinquish whatever food they are carrying.

Few, if any, frigatebirds have nested successfully on the mainland of Ascension for two centuries, but with the recent eradication of cats there is every hope that they will soon return. And, with luck, other birds will join them: Masked Boobies, Red-billed Tropicbirds, Brown Noddies, all seabird species that were once common on the mainland, but are today confined to the safety of Boatswainbird, and a few other offshore stacks.

Circling the vertical walls of Boatswainbird in a small boat, it is possible to imagine how Ascension must have looked four centuries ago. Great wheels of frigatebirds hang in the thermals above the island, while lines of boobies stream in from their distant feeding grounds. It is simultaneously a breathtaking spectacle and a poignant reminder of what has been lost.

Landing on the island is prohibited in an effort to minimize disturbance to nesting birds, but it was not always so. The thick beds of phosphate-rich guano these birds produced did not escape the notice of 19th century island residents, and as early as 1851, people scaled the cliffs of Boatswainbird to gather it. It was useful, of course, as fertilizer

Black Noddies nest along tiny ledges at the base of Boatswainbird Island. With the eradication of cats on Ascension, this may be one of the first species to re-colonize main island.

for the island gardens, but it was also shipped back to England for sale. On and off for the next 80 years, several people tried to make a business out of it, amid some of the hardest working conditions imaginable, but with little or no success.

On the mainland of Ascension, meanwhile, only one bird, the Sooty Tern, managed to hold its own in the face of cat predation, largely through the sheer force of numbers. Known on Ascension as the Wideawake, (a delightful bit of onomatopoeia which suggests the birds' shrill three-note call) the Sooty Terns still gather every year in large, crowded colonies, called 'Fairs', presumably because of their endless, round-the-clock activity.

Sooties are handsome birds: streamlined, elegant, and intensely social. But like most colonial birds, packed closely together, they often seem unreconciled to the proximity of their neighbours. No wonder that there is rarely a quiet moment in a Wideawake Fair. At all hours of the day, the air is filled with an unending chorus of screeching meant to express everything from annoyance to affection, all in precisely the same tone of voice.

The colonial habit may at times be disagreeable, but it was also the Wideawakes' salvation, for only these massive gatherings of tightly packed birds allowed them to survive the relentless slaughter by feral cats. In the 1950s, when it was estimated that 750,000 terns nested on the island, as many as 5% of them were killed and eaten by cats every season – a total of 37,500 birds. But terns are long-lived birds, and an annual loss of "only" 5%, although horrific, did not destroy the colony.

This may have also forced the birds to synchronize their breeding in an attempt to reduce the risk of being eaten. Simply said, there is safety in numbers. Although Sooty

An avian high-rise, Boatswainbird Island has been a vital refuge for nesting seabirds, free from the rats and cats that have decimated the once-great mainland colonies. Today, it is the only nesting place in the world for the endemic Ascension Frigatebird.

Terns elsewhere in the world breed all through the year, the birds on Ascension have a unique breeding cycle of every 9.6 months. Every year, the process starts in a different month. This suggests that their breeding cycle is less tied to the availability of food, than to two centuries of predation by cats. In essence, they breed as often as they can – a macabre sort of insurance against what, for many, would be a short life.

And if the prospect of being eaten by cats were not bad enough, Wideawakes also faced a longstanding tradition of egg collecting on Ascension. 19th century garrison records suggest that the marines on the island were inordinately fond of fresh eggs: as many as 120,000 were collected in a single week in the 1830s. Even as recently as the 1950s, up to ten thousand were taken every season for local consumption or sent to friends and relatives on St. Helena. It has been outlawed since the 1960s.

To add insult to injury, when the US Army built their new runway in 1942, they chose the obvious – some say the only – flat place on the island, called Waterloo Plain. Inconveniently, this was also the favourite nesting area of Sooty Terns.

No one seriously suggested abandoning the plans for the new runway, seen as crucial to the war effort. Instead, an American ornithologist named James Chapin, was hired to provide a solution. His answer was simple: destroy all the eggs at the start of the season and encourage the birds to move elsewhere. It worked; US soldiers methodically smashed 40,000 eggs and the runway was completed on time. And, as predicted, the terns dutifully moved on to other, less desirable, nesting sites. (After all this, I find it extraordinary that any terns at all remain on Ascension; I feel certain that if they'd had anywhere else to go, they would have abandoned the island long ago.)

Before the construction of the runway in 1942 nesting Wideawakes covered every inch of the Waterloo Plain.

My favourite bird on Ascension, meanwhile, is another tern - a cousin to the Wideawake, but vastly different in both appearance and temperament. This is the Fairy Tern, a delicate creature whose light, buoyant flight makes it seem more like a butterfly than a seabird. And unlike Wideawakes, which can be argumentative on occasion, Fairy Terns are sweet natured and surprisingly curious.

On Ascension, Fairy Terns are most common among the tall groves of eucalyptus trees that line the upper Ramps, the switch backed road that leads from Two Boats to the top of Green Mountain. Here, where cool breezes rustle the branches, these wide-eyed fairies nest in the crooks of trees, or on impossibly thin twigs. No nest is built; the egg is simply laid directly onto whatever flat spot the bird can find, and held in place by the brooding adult.

The exotic trees and shrubbery of Green Mountain also provide a home for some of Ascension's land birds, among them small flocks of African Canaries, and Common Waxbills, both introduced to the island in the 19th century. Many other species were brought to Ascension over the years, some for their songs, and others in an effort to control insects that were wreaking havoc in the island's vegetable garden.

These introductions met with mixed success. The birds did little to reduce garden pests, and most simply couldn't fine enough to eat. Starlings, thrushes, owls and Jackdaws were all imported, but none have survived. In the end, only Indian Mynas and a few House Sparrows, brought to the island as recently as 1986, have become established in small numbers.

Several game birds were brought to the island for sport in the 19th century, including pheasants and guinea fowl, but they did not last long. Another one did, however: the Red-necked

Sooty terns feed primarily on flying fish and squid, which they catch on the wing, following schools of predatory tuna.   They are one of the most abundant seabirds in tropical seas worldwide.

A young Sooty Tern gets no marks for beauty. Still unable to fly, it has little to do except to wait for food to arrive. Soon, however, it will be off on its own, facing the rigours of life at sea.

Nearly full-size, a young Sooty Tern begs for food from its parent. These birds breed every 9 and a half months, so are gone from the island only briefly every year.

Incubating can be boring, even for a Booby. On a small offshore stack, this Brown Booby entertains itself with an old feather while waiting for its mate to return from the sea.

A Brown Noddy stands guard over its young chick, perhaps one of the first to successfully hatch on the main island in nearly two hundred years: cause for celebration.

There is no mistaking frigatebirds in flight, with their forked tails and angular wings. These soaring frigates are returning to Boatswainbird for the night, likely after a day of making miserable the lives of other birds.

Francolin, a native of Africa. Today, their surprisingly loud, rhythmic calls can still be heard for great distances, especially in Grazing Valley, below the western cliffs of Green Mountain.

The handful of exotic birds that have managed to find a home on Ascension, however, are little consolation for the loss of the massive colonies of seabirds which were once among the island's greatest treasures. But with the eradication of cats, the re-colonization of Ascension has already begun. Almost immediately after the last cats were removed, a few pairs of Masked Boobies began nesting on the main island: more are certain to follow.

One of my most memorable afternoons on Ascension was spent on a long hike over the lava fields near English Bay in search of nesting seabirds. After an hour or more of scrambling over some very unfriendly terrain we finally reached the edge of the sea, grateful for the sudden slight breeze, and a chance to rest.

Nearby, on a small rocky ledge, we found what we had come to see: a single adult Brown Noddy, tending to a tiny ball of fluff that cowered between its feet. This little Noddy chick, wide-eyed and irresistible, may have been the first of its kind to be born on the mainland of Ascension in nearly two hundred years. What's more, it should have every chance of surviving to adulthood, and raising a family of its own.

Some day soon, perhaps within a decade or less, the ghosts of Ascension will be banished, and the long-empty lava fields filled once more with the chaotic, raucous – and wonderful – sounds of birds. Nothing would please me more.

A baby turtle rises for its first breath after being taken by the sea. He'd better be quick about it – there is almost certainly a hungry frigatebird waiting overhead for just such an opportunity.

Afterword - The Future

As I write these words, in late 2004, Ascension Island is on the brink of what may be its most significant transformation since the British Navy first took possession in 1815: a change from company town to true community. In just the past year, the first representative government has been established to allow island residents to have a voice in their own future. In addition, private land ownership is becoming a real possibility for the first time.

Ascension society has long been an odd mixture of military and civilian, of nationalities, missions and attitudes. Nearly everyone on the island is on temporary contract, many for no more than two years at a time. The result has been a largely transient population, many people just marking their time while waiting to move on to somewhere else. For that reason, the island has never enjoyed the same sort of continuity that exists in some, more settled, communities. People come and go, but few have a sense of permanence.

While I was on Ascension, I spoke to a man who had lived on the island for seven years, during which time he had never been for a hike on any of the island's fine trails. Like many people working here, he did his job, enjoyed his salary and the material comforts of life on the American base – and looked forward to the day when he could leave.

Other people, though, have thrived on Ascension, and have lived here for twenty years or more. They have chosen to stay for many reasons, among them the proximity to nature, the many outdoor activities, as well as the personal attachments that can develop in a small, isolated community like this. For people with the right attitude, it can be a wonderful place to live, a haven for families and a marvellous place to bring up children, safe and essentially crime-free.

Still, the future of Ascension is not entirely clear. It is unlikely to ever become entirely self-sufficient, but may evolve into a blend of private and public interests. The licensing of offshore fishing rights, for example, could bring significant income to the island, but that would require considerable investment to provide the necessary enforcement. Tourism is also seen as a potential source of income, with sport fishing and wildlife viewing as the major draws. But will people travel to this far-flung island to see turtles and seabirds, catch some fish - and soak up some Napoleonic history?

I hope so, because Ascension has much to offer anyone who gives her a chance. Though neither an unaltered wilderness nor a typical vision of a tropical paradise, it is, like all islands, utterly unique.

Photo Notes

The rewards for a photographer on Ascension are enormous. The striking landscape offers surprising diversity, and the wildlife is, of course, superb. I was delighted to have opportunity to spend my days there in the company of thousands of nesting terns, and my nights alongside gigantic turtles. I also managed to hike many of the island's many fine trails and discover some of its secret corners.

Having said that, I didn't always find the working conditions easy. I was quickly reminded, for example, that the beautiful light of dawn and dusk - light that gladdens the heart of every photographer - is maddeningly brief at this latitude. Often by eight in the morning it was either too sunny for decent pictures or too hot to be outside taking them! This compressed nearly my entire picture taking into as little as half an hour at either end of the day; the rest of my time was largely devoted to sitting in front of an electric fan and drinking vast quantities of water.

Lurking in the back of my mind, all the while, was the nagging pressure of time. With less than three weeks on Ascension, I found it impossible to see or photograph everything, or to do it as well as I would have wished. I simply left far too many pictures untaken. I did, however, enjoy the sense of discovery of being among the first professional photographers to work here. I have always found it much more satisfying, and more fun, to interpret a place without having my mind already filled with lots of other people's pictures.

In the end, I am happy with what I was able to capture on film, and plagued by what I missed. I suppose it will always be so: absolute contentment is beyond the reach of the creative mind.

On the technical side, the photographs in this book were almost entirely taken with Nikon F100 cameras and an assortment of lenses, large and small. The only exception to this was a handful of shots taken underwater with the Nikonos amphibious camera. My continuing film of choice is Fuji Velvia, because of its rich saturated colours, and fine detail. (Although I have begun toying with digital cameras, I did not use them at all on this project.)

Finally, in a world where the inherent power of photography is being sadly undermined by the ease and universality of digital manipulation - I think it is important to state that all of the pictures in this book represent real moments in nature. None have been created on the computer, manipulated or fundamentally altered in any way other than a few very minor adjustments of brightness, colour and cropping, usually making up for mistakes I made in the first place!

Kevin Schafer
October 2004

Not every trip ashore ends up with a successful nest. Human disturbance, lights, dogs – in other words, almost anything – can cause a female turtle to abandon the effort and return to the seas without nesting. *Long Beach*.

Ascension Island

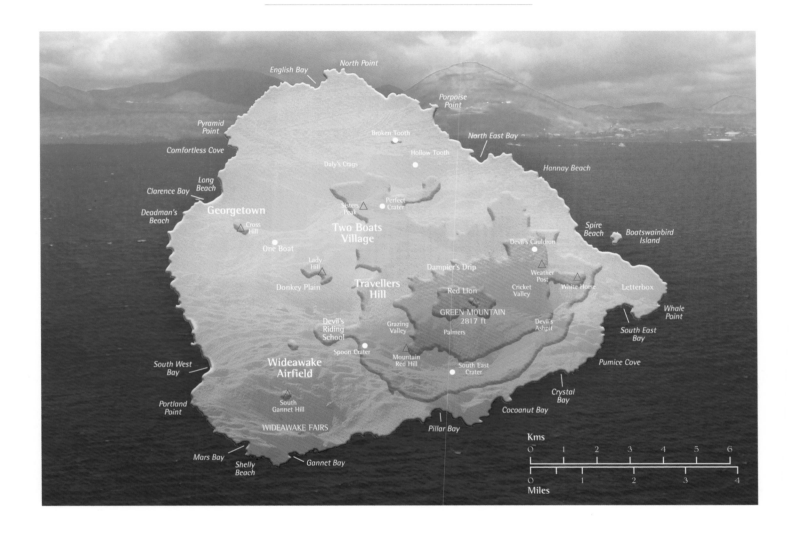

Bibliography & Links

Ascension makes a powerful impression on nearly everyone fortunate enough to visit her. It should not be surprising, then, that there is a copious amount of published material, far beyond what you might expect for such a remote and rarely visited corner of the globe.

The following were among my sources for this volume:

Ashmole,
Philip and Myrtle
St. Helena and Ascension Island:
A Natural History.
(Anthony Nelson, 2000)

The bible of Ascension natural history, this relatively new book is packed with information on every aspect of the island's flora and fauna. It is an essential reference for anyone with a serious interest in these islands.

Darwin, Charles
Voyage of the Beagle
(Modern Library, 2001)

Darwin devotes only three and a half pages to Ascension, which he visited for four days in July of 1836. He devotes most of that space to his first love, geology.

Ghione, Sergio
Turtle Island
(Thomas Dunne / St. Martin's Press, 2003)

An Italian doctor joins a turtle research expedition on Ascension. This book combines information on sea turtles with the author's amusing reflections on island life.

Hart-Davis, Duff
Ascension : The Story of a South Atlantic Island.
(Constable & Co. 1972)

Now thirty years old, this remains the most authoritative history of British presence on Ascension, written by a young British journalist.

Packer, John
The Ascension Island Handbook
(Ascension Heritage Society, 2002)

First published in 1968, this simple booklet is a treasure trove of island information, with details on plants, geology, history – and the origin of place names.

Stonehouse,
Bernard
Wideawake Island.
(Hutchinson & Co., 1960)

This is the story of the British Ornithological Union's eighteen-month expedition to Ascension in 1957, during which they studied the birds of the island in more detail than ever before.

Weaver, Barry
A Guide to the Geology of Ascension Island and Saint Helena.
(Self-published, 2002)

A detailed introduction to the geology of both Atlantic Ocean Islands. Much of this information is also available at the author's website: **http://geowww.ou. edu/~bweaver/Ascension/ai.htm**

Links

Besides the books listed, there is considerable general information about Ascension available on the Internet. Among the most useful sites are:

Ascension Conservation:　　**www.conservation.org.ac**
Ascension Government :　　**www.ascension-island.gov.ac**
Ascension Heritage Society:　　**www.heritage.org.ac**

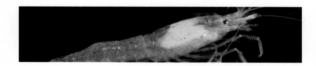

Ascension Links Page:
www.websmith.demon.co.uk/ascensionisland/links.htm

Marine Turtle Research Group: **www.seaturtle.org/mtrg/**

To contact the author, please feel free to visit:
www.kevinschafer.com

To contact the publisher or purchase additional copies visit:
www.coachhouseonline.co.uk

Huge lava blocks – known as the "Sugar Cubes" – line one side of Grazing Valley, at the foot of mist-shrouded Green Mountain. To dismiss the rock on Ascension as simply "volcanic" is to ignore the remarkable variety of forms it assumes.

The moon rises over Sisters Peak at dusk, viewed from Long Beach.

An agave flower stalk is silhouetted against a fiery sunset,
from Travellers Hill.